Skateboarding:

CRAILSLIDES TO WALLRIDES

Skateboarding:
CRAILSLIDES TO WALLRIDES

Evan Goodfellow

Photography by:

Tadashi Yamaoda

www.tadashiphoto.com
www.cobrahmagazine.com

Tricks performed by:

Evan Goodfellow

Tadashi Yamaoda

Bruce Tucker

and friends

Veva Skateboard Books

Oakland, California

Skateboarding:
CRAILSLIDES TO WALLRIDES

Evan Goodfellow

Photos: Tadashi Yamaoda

Veva Skateboard Books Ltd.
886 Pine St. # B, Oakland, CA 94607

Acknowledgements

Thanks to the following:

Cover Design and Layout:

Daryll Peirce at Art Derailed
www.artderailed.com

Cover Photos:

WISDA
www.nickwisda.com
Front Cover: Tom Geilfus
Back Cover: Tyler Franz

Editors:

Graham Emde
Trent Young
Charse Yun

Veva Skateboard Books Ltd.

To stay in touch with the author, check out his personal skateboard blog at:
www.goneskateboarding.blogspot.com

I dedicate this book to my friends and family.

Thanks for your support.

Preface

This is my fifth instructional skateboarding book and it was the hardest for me to sit down and write by far. When Tadashi and I began planning for this book close to two years ago, we came up with lists of unusual tricks and then debated whether a certain trick was worthy of being in the book. In the end, we crossed out a lot of tricks. I wrestled with the question of whether the tricks we chose would still be popular ten years from now or be gone forever, never to return.

The goal of each book I write is to have tricks that are still going to be staple skateboarding tricks ten, maybe even twenty years down the road. We know certain tricks like the kickflip, heelflip and 180's will be here to stay. They are resistant to fads. They can be built upon to create new tricks and they have become the building blocks of the sport. Other tricks will probably never come back. A perfect example of a trick that didn't make the cut is pressure flips. The reason why I didn't include pressure flips in this book is because it doesn't involve an ollie and it can't really be added to or taken to bigger obstacles. Not to mention the trick looks sinfully ugly when performed.

Hopefully the tricks selected in this book will help the reader to increase their bag of tricks so that they can continue to get better at skateboarding and continue to create new variations off the tricks that already exist. In order for skateboarding to thrive and progress, skateboarders need to create new tricks and new ways of doing tricks, and they need to do these tricks on differing obstacles and differing terrain. The people I chose in the history portion of this book are skateboarders who broke away from the mainstream when it came to their video parts and magazine coverage. They dared to try different tricks from what everyone else was doing at the time regardless of any looming fear that they might not be cool or might be ridiculed.

May you enjoy this book and continue to keep skating and learning new tricks.

Sincerely,
Evan Goodfellow

Warning Label:

Skateboarding is an extremely dangerous sport. Riders should wear safety equipment at all times and should not try anything that is dangerous or beyond their ability. Although riders in the book do not wear safety equipment, they are trained professionals. This book in no way endorses skateboarding without the use of proper safety equipment.

Contents

Introduction

Many skateboarders around the world specialize in certain areas of skateboarding. Some skateboarders are particularly good at vert skating, others at riding ledges, while still others specialize in rails or flip tricks. Being a talented skateboarder is no easy task. You have to practice hours on end and devote yourself to keeping up-to-date with the newest tricks and styles.

After skateboarding for an extended period of time, I came to realize that skateboarding tricks get recycled. Some tricks are brought back from the archives and made cool again after years of not being seen or thought about, only to lose their popularity nearly as quickly as they had regained it. Some tricks unfortunately are never brought back. Close to ten years ago, bluntslides and nosebluntslides were almost completely erased from the memory of modern skateboarders when they saw a sudden resurgence in popularity because of skateboarders who expanded on them with new tricks like nollies. Several years ago, I was shocked when I saw what I thought was impossible: someone did a nollie kickflip to nosebluntslide. Another way bluntslides were popularized again was skateboarders who did them down huge ledges or rails. One individual who did this was Heath Kirchart when he did a frontside bluntslide down the massive hubba at UC Irvine.

The secret to keeping skateboarding vibrant is through innovation and the continual challenge to do things that seem close to impossible. In the early 90's, skateboarding saw a serious decline in participants due to the fact that people were getting bored with the sport. At that time, ramp skating was the common theme and 98 percent of photos that were featured in skateboard magazines were done on vert. Skateboarders revived the sport by adapting it and creating new challenges through street skating. If skateboarding is going to continue on for another twenty years, there is going to have to be a continual challenge for skateboarders to grow and progress. The avenues of progression are getting wider and wider as many tricks have been invented in the past ten years and done on a varied assortment of obstacles such as curbs, rails, ramps, flat ground, pools, walls, off huge ramps and even over the Great Wall of China!

Where do the tricks go and how do they become out of style? Just as in the world of fashion, some tricks become out of date and unstylish. The professionals and amateurs of the top skateboarding companies set the styles by the tricks they choose. In many ways they are the gatekeepers of what is cool for both the obstacles and tricks that people skate. If the average skateboarder doesn't see the pros doing certain tricks, he will assume that those tricks are out of style and will therefore stop trying those tricks. The reason why skateboard tricks are always changing is because pros want to continually do harder tricks to keep their competitive edge and thus ensure their place in the skateboard industry.

Where the Weirdest of the Weird Show Up

The game of S-K-A-T-E seems to be the place where people bring the strangest tricks out on display. I worked at a skate park for several summers during college and not a day passed when I wouldn't be challenged by a little up-and-comer to play S-K-A-T-E as a way of testing their ability against a more senior skateboarder. Sometimes these young skateboarders would have all the newest tricks down and would be able to do some tricks that I couldn't. In such cases, when my reputation was on the line and all my modern tricks were exhausted, I would reach back into the recesses of my bag of tricks, and pull out an old trick that had gone out of style long ago; in almost every case I would win the game. The reason I won was that they had never seen the trick and certainly didn't know how to do it. These tricks included impossibles, late-shuvits, back foot flips or other tricks.

The reason why I wanted to write this book is because some tricks don't fit into specific categories like flip tricks, rails, ramps or curb tricks. Some tricks are on the border between categories. Maybe they could be termed "old school," meaning they were done in the past but have resurfaced and been included in modern day skateboarding. An example of this would be a trick like wallrides. It is important to learn these tricks, as they will

> **Doing only the coolest tricks can get boring real fast, but doing tricks that are fun and unique will add to your style and make others take notice of you.**

help not only when you are playing a game of S-K-A-T-E, but also because they can add some originality to your skating. Doing only the coolest tricks can get boring real fast, but doing tricks that are fun and unique will add to your style and make others take notice of you.

Thinking back on the parts that were the most groundbreaking in the history of skate videos, it became evident that they weren't derived from run-of-the-mill pros or ams doing the latest fad tricks. The most memorable parts for me were of skateboarders who showed originality and did unique tricks that were out of the ordinary. One video in particular that stuck out was "P.J. Ladd's Wonderful Horrible Life." His part was revolutionary because he did combos and tricks that shocked everyone. "P.J. Ladd's Wonderful Horrible Life" came out after the Osiris phase which was still in the minds of a lot people at the time. That phase ruined technical skating with its multiple flip-in flip-out tricks and the problems posed by baggy jeans and big fat puffy shoes.

When the video first came out, the owner of the shop I rode for called me at my house and said that I had to come in right away to watch it. He told me how this new rider P.J. Ladd was going to blow my mind. I asked what his forte was, guessing that he skated big crazy stairs like so many other pros at the time. My friend replied, "He's super technical, but in an amazing way. Plus he can skate big stuff, too." I was a little hesitant but when I saw the video my view totally changed. P.J. Ladd had created his own new tricks and combinations that left me wanting to immediately go skate to see if maybe, just maybe, I could learn one of his new tricks.

The Spirit of Innovation

While making this book, Tadashi and I travelled around from spot to spot to find some unusual things to skate with the help of our tour guide Bruce. Out of all the spots we went to, the one that was most memorable was this spot in Vancouver, B.C., Canada called Leeside. Tadashi flew up from Oakland and we only had a week to shoot the photos, but in Vancouver rain stops for no one. Seeking shelter from the rain, we went to this place called Leeside, which was created by a skateboarder named Lee Matasi. He was a typical skateboard addict who wanted to skate year round. But to do so in Vancouver, where it almost never stops raining during winter, he had to make his spot under a bridge. His spot originally consisted of only a rail, some makeshift boxes and whatever he could drag out or make under the bridge.

In December 2005, Lee Matasi was shot and killed by some random gang violence that caught him in the wrong place at the wrong time. Since his death, the skateboarders of Vancouver wanted to make his little makeshift skate park better as a memorial and tribute to him. Since his death, they have poured cement quarter pipes up to the wall as well as added some legit ramps and ledges. Local graffiti artists also dedicated a mural portrait of Lee on one of the walls in memory of him.

When I first visited the spot I stood there. I heard about his tragic death and I thought about how he had started making this spot with nothing but an open dirty space. He had made something amazing out of it. The spot was perfect for skateboarding because of all the fun wallrides and banks to ledges. Unfortunately, many of the photos shot here didn't turn out that well due to the fact that it was under a bridge and the flashes were bouncing around off the cement walls, floors and underside of the bridge.

Location as an Influence

Before videos came out so often and professional skateboarders travelled from country to country to film, it was where you lived that seemed to have a greater influence on your sense of style, the types of obstacles you used and the tricks that you did. Back then it wasn't so much where in the world you were from but where in the United States you were from—East Coast, West Coast, North or South. Thinking back with nostalgia, I still remember to this day when the East Coast video "Zero: Eastern Exposure" came out. The video was out of control. It followed guys skating through the busy streets of New York and Philadelphia, not just skating a spot but making the whole city a spot. You could tell the streets weren't smooth like in California. The wheels they rode were bigger so they could maneuver on the rough ground and the tricks were amazing—tons of wallrides and pole jams.

Another place in the U.S. that really differed from the Los Angeles vibe was San Francisco back when the heart of skateboarding lived there. There was a spot called the EMB or Embarcadero, which was located right across the street from Pier 7 and right by Hubba Hideout. This spot spawned a whole style of skateboarding and tricks. Individuals around the globe watched the videos of people skating EMB and emulated their moves and their style.

Ed Templeton

Ed Templeton runs a blog that I seem to find myself on every morning before work. It is full of his humorous reflections on life, skateboarding, and people. The blog has two parts to it. The first is called Toy Machine and features skate photos and the riders' daily lives captured by a point-and-shoot digital camera. The second part deals with Ed's art and travels. The other day there was a link to one of his upcoming art shows in Europe and on the website there was a brief summary of Ed Templeton's life. It told how he was born in 1972 and grew up in Orange County until his family moved to a trailer park in Corona. That's where his father ran off with his babysitter and Ed moved with his mom to Huntington Beach. The summary was so succinct and strangely tragic that it almost sounded comical, like an episode from "My Name is Earl."

But his story is true, and the story has a bright side. It was in Huntington Beach that Ed

Ed brought back two almost forgotten tricks and added to them, showing everyone that old tricks could still be cool.

fell in love with skateboarding and went on to get sponsored and become a major influence in the skateboard world. As a young kid I remember seeing Ed in various skateboard magazines and videos. He has always stood out to me as one of the great trendsetters in skateboarding and skateboard tricks. He has continually done tricks in contests and videos that weren't "cool" at the time but later became cool.

One trick I will always associate with him is bluntslides. Once he won first place at a contest in Vancouver back in about 1994 with this awesome run he had. In the run he gapped a fun box to noseblunt slide down a hubba. The gap was huge and he was pushing so fast in order to land in noseblunt on the other side. Another trick he did during the contest was an impossible tail grab over the pyramid hip. Impossibles used to be really cool back in the early 90's and they were dubbed impossibles due to how hard they were to do back then. Boards were heavy and the average trick wasn't popped very high, so it was hard to get high enough to wrap it around your foot. By the time of the contest the trick had faded into the background and was rarely done. Here, Ed brought back two almost forgotten tricks and added to them, showing everyone that old tricks could still be cool.

Ed Templeton began riding for New Deal back in 1990 and stayed on for two years. He then started a company with Mike Vallely called Television, which didn't last very long. Next, he created his own company called Toy Machine in 1993. Toy Machine has had its shares of ups and downs, but was seriously up in 1996 when it was widely considered the best skateboard company around. Chad Muska and Jamie Thomas rode for them. Their fame was peaking when Toy Machine released "Welcome to Hell." Chad Muska had a part in the video, but after a fight at the premier of the video Chad quit and pulled his part before the video hit skate shops. Chad promptly switched teams to Shorty's, and his footage, which was originally shot for "Welcome to Hell," later appeared in their first video.

Not only is Ed an outstanding skateboarder, but he is also a talented artist with paintings and photos displayed in galleries around the world. Art is not an uncommon interest among skateboarders. This creativity within Ed has likely helped him to come up with so many great video parts. Even as Ed has gotten older it seems his parts have become more creative. Older pros like Ed have a hard time competing with big tricks down stairs and rails and therefore have to become more creative by doing fresh new tricks that have yet to be seen.

Chris Haslam

To me, Chris Haslam is going to be one of skateboarding's greatest contributors for new tricks. The reason why is because his talent and ability are unprecedented. He can do almost anything he wants to on a skateboard and is not afraid to try new tricks that might be mocked or laughed at because of the way they look. He seems to not take image too seriously, especially in regard to skateboard tricks. Some tricks in his previous video parts have been goofy, completely unseen before, and amazing. His combination of talent and unconventional thinking lead him to create new tricks and advance skateboarding in a way that many professionals simply can't.

The first time I saw Chris Haslam skate was before his video parts in "Almost Round 3" and "Cheese and Crackers." I was staying at a friend's in Vancouver and we headed over to the Richmond skateboard park. My friend had been telling me about Chris Haslam, who at the time, had just gotten sponsored by the skateboard company called Deca. We got to the park and as I started warming up I noticed a guy just cruising around the park and popping huge airs on the quarter pipe. Later that night, he began riding the mini and I sat down to watch. I don't think he missed one trick. He would do really long difficult runs and when he stopped it was simply because he was too tired. His runs included nollie k grinds, switch back tailslides and other really tech tricks performed with speed and fluency.

My friend explained to me how Chris Haslam would show up at the Richmond park near his house and skate for eight hours a day without taking long breaks to sit around. That is how he honed his amazing skills. His part in the "Almost: Round 3" was amazing. One of his most innovative tricks on this video was a k grind nollie flip pop over, on a flat bar. After the "Almost" video came "Cheese and Crackers" which was mini ramp madness. His part included amazing tricks like a nose-blunt nollie flip out, a blunt triple flip out, and an overcrooks nollie flip out.

If you watch the old Osiris videos you'll notice that although they were really tech and crazy at the time they really lacked style; after a short time the whole Osiris style became a joke. Haslam's video parts are technical but differ from the Osiris fad because he skates fast, and pops his tricks high. His style fits with the skating of today. He has complimented his ability with his style and shown us that skateboarders can take the sport to new insane levels and look good doing it.

Ali Boulala

Ali Boulala was born January 28, 1979 in Stockholm, Sweden and is sponsored by Flip Skateboards and Osiris Shoes. On March 6, 2007 he was in a motorcycle accident that killed his good friend Shane Cross. Ali himself barely escaped with his life, and his doctors were forced to put him into a medically induced coma because of the severity of his injuries. Now that he has somewhat recovered, he faces a jail sentence that could last until 2012. When thinking of people who have contributed to the development of a new way of skating, I felt I had to choose Ali due to his unusual skateboard video parts. He has garnered criticism due to his unusual tricks and the objects he chooses to skate, not to mention his overly flamboyant clothing.

Ali Boulala became famous through his various parts in the Baker and Flip videos. To some, his fashion seemed to take precedence over his skateboarding ability. His billowing pirate shirts and extremely tight pants all added to his rock star persona that made him famous both on and off the skateboard. This is not to say that his skateboarding was by any means sub-par. It was unusual for sure, but equally amazing. In his "Flip Sorry" video part he tried to ollie a 25 stair in France. In his early skateboarding days he was known for ollieing and doing tricks down large staircases. His more recent footage is of him skating unusual ledges and doing uncommon tricks down or across what normally might not be skated or even looked at.

Daewon Song

Daewon Song was born February 19, 1975 in Seoul, South Korea. He was raised in America and was sponsored in the early days of World Industries. Out of all the guys I researched for this book, I was most shocked by Daewon. I thought I knew a lot about him. I knew he liked to do manuals and that he was more technical in his skating than almost any professional in the industry. I thought that in his old age Daewon would skate less and be more involved with running his skateboard company Almost. The reality, however, proved to be quite the opposite.

As I read through interviews with him over the years I realized that he was only fourteen when the evil empire of World Industries sponsored him. By evil I mean the owner had relatively no morals and was always doing things to shock the skateboard community; that man was Steve Rocco. To shock a bunch of teenagers is hard work but to shock a community that the general public already considers rebels was even harder. Rocco was able to shock almost anyone. Daewon recalls the crazy parties at the company and the complete lack of restraint within the company. The company was making loads of money and the young underaged riders were free to run wild provided they kept producing good skateboarding. One summer, Daewon failed a class and had to inform his boss that he was going to be taking summer school classes and couldn't go on tour. His boss Rocco pulled him aside to give him some advice. Rocco explained how he had dropped out of high school and was now super rich and drove a Porsche. He told Daewon to forget summer school and come on tour. Daewon agreed and went on tour.

The thing that surprised me was that throughout Daewon's various interviews, he seemed so lighthearted and didn't take things too seriously, especially regarding himself and money. He won the Thrasher Magazine award in 2008 for Skater of the Year and seemed to make fun of those in the industry who were all about the money. Reading about Daewon, I soon realized that he didn't win the award due to his natural talent but more because of his hard work. His skateboarding schedule begins when he wakes up; as he lays in bed, he begins thinking of what tricks he wants to learn that day, and then after going for donuts and coffee he is off for a full day of skateboarding. He said he starts in the morning and is done by about 9 or 10 p.m. For most pros that is unheard of. He remarked that he does it because he loves it and because he feels like there are always more tricks to learn.

When commenting on the progression of skateboarding, he stated that the mid-90's seemed to be the most innovative time in skateboarding to him. It was like there were new tricks always being created and that you always felt like you were learning something new. Daewon's innovations didn't stop in the mid-90's though; you can go on Youtube or try and get your hands on his old videos such as "Rodney vs. Daewon" which were huge hits and demonstrated his technical abilities. More recent videos include his mini-ramp video "Cheese and Crackers" which he did with Chris Haslam. When you see that video, you spend half the time trying to figure out what

When you see that video, you spend half the time trying to figure out what the trick would be called and how it is even humanly possible.

the trick would be called and how it is even humanly possible. Daewon Song has been around for a long time and with his awesome attitude and love for skateboarding he should prove to be around for even longer.

Ricky Oyola

To me, Ricky Oyola embodied the East Coast style that came out in the late 90's in videos such as "Eastern Exposure." They cruised through the city and skated really rough terrain that was so different than anything you saw in California. You were seeing people skate rough cement and use metal grated plates propped up by bricks as ramps. The skating was raw and I am sure if the spots were as smooth and perfect as the spots seen in California, they wouldn't have been half as interesting.

Ricky Oyola attributes his style of skating the whole city like one big skate park to the fact that when he was younger he would park his car in West Philly and then skate for blocks and blocks to meet up with people, the whole while hitting up spots along the way.

Guy Mariano

Guy Mariano was born in 1977 and got sponsored by Blind Skateboards at the age of 14. He then began to ride for Girl Skateboards from which he retired in 1997 after his epic part in the "Mouse" video. His ability to create new tricks and take them to the next level, whether switch or regular, was unbelievable. One of the tricks that highlighted his amazing ability at that time was his switch backside tailslide down a six-stair rail in Vancouver in the friend's section of the 1995 Chocolate video.

Recently, he came out of retirement and once again quickly rose to his previous status, if not higher. He first began with a Thrasher interview and then went on to have several pictures in Transworld and The Skateboard Mag before going on to have one of the best, if not the best, sections in the Lakai video "Beware the Flare." One of his most innovative tricks from this video was a nosebluntslide nollie 360 heelflip shuvit out. He also wowed skateboarders everywhere with his ability to flip out of grinds and slides.

While speculations circulate as to why exactly Guy Mariano retired, the answer seems to revolve around injury and addiction. He has alluded to this in his recent interviews but has always steered clear of getting into specifics. Now Guy seems to be in a solid place, focusing on his skateboarding as well as his personal life, and free from addiction and distractions. He has also been getting involved in filming, the most notable instance being his help with the production of the recent Lakai video.

> **His ability to create new tricks and take them to the next level, whether switch or regular, was unbelievable.**

Eric Koston

Eric Koston is Thai-American. His father was serving in the Air Force when he met his mother in Thailand. Eric was born in Bangkok and then moved to San Bernardino, California when he was nine months old. Koston has stayed at the height of the skateboard industry for the past thirteen years. By "height" I mean that he has literally gone unrivaled in every video part he has come out with, whether for Girl, ES, or Lakai.

> **Koston's fame is due to his ability to make insane combinations of already existing tricks and do them on equally insane objects.**

It may seem like blasphemy to say, but I wouldn't consider Koston a huge innovator of new tricks compared to someone like Rodney Mullen who invented numerous tricks that are being done now. Koston's fame is due to his ability to make insane combinations of already existing tricks and do them on equally insane objects.

Koston has stayed innovative because of how he takes new or old tricks and takes them to the next level. A good example of this is his last trick on the Girl video "Yeah Right," which he incidentally filmed the night before all the footage had to be in; he performed a 360 flip nosebluntslide down a handrail. At that time, the trick had rarely been seen on anything but a curb and certainly not down a rail. Another famous trick he did was a switch frontside 360 bigspin to switch backside bluntslide down a rail.

Change is Good

There have been too many influential skateboarders to mention every single person who has contributed to the development of unique styles and tricks. The ones that were mentioned stand out right now for this period of time in skateboarding, but within several years there will surely be new innovators within the sport. Skateboarding needs this fresh blood to keep it exciting and evolving so that ten years from now the sport will continue to thrive. Skateboarding differs from other sports like baseball and tennis because those sports are stationary—the rules of those games do not change much and have stood the test of time. Skateboarding, on the other hand, is still relatively new and its popularity has expanded over the years as the sport has experienced great changes and innovations. May skateboarding continue to evolve and grow in popularity and continue to offer the excitement that got me on a board over twenty years ago.

Trick Tips

Frontside Wallride

Ride up to the wall at a 45-degree angle with your front facing the wall. Place your front foot two inches below the bottom bolts on your front truck with your toes an inch away from the edge of the board. Place your back foot flat across the tail of the board. When the nose of the board

nears the wall, jam or slide your back foot against the wall and lift up slightly with your tail. When the front wheels of the board hit the wall, bend your front leg. Keep pushing your back foot towards the wall so the back wheels hit the wall. When your wheels hit the wall, begin turning

The secret is to practice riding up a steep banked ramp. It will be good practice for jamming your back wheels into the ramp and making the arc.

before you reach the height of your wall ride. Turn your front foot and push your back foot up and around so that it follows an arc. When the front wheels near the ground, lean back on the tail and prepare for leveling out as you hit the ground.

Backside Wallride

Ride up to the wall at a 45-degree angle with your back facing the wall. Place your front foot two inches below the bottom bolts on your front truck with your toes an inch away from the edge of the board. Place your back foot flat across the tail of the board. When the nose of the board nears

the wall, jam or slide your back foot against the wall and lift up slightly with your tail. When the front wheels of the board hit the wall, bend your front leg. Keep pushing with your back foot so the back wheels hit the wall. When all four wheels hit the wall, begin turning before you reach the

The secret is to practice riding up a steep banked ramp. It will be good practice for jamming your back wheels into the ramp and making the arc.

height of your wall ride. Turn your front foot and push your back foot up and around so that it follows an arc. When the front wheels near the ground, lean back on the tail and prepare for leveling out as you land on the flat ground. As both wheels make contact shift your weight and ride away.

37

Wallride to Fakie

Ride straight up to the wall. Have your front foot over
the top bolts of your front truck. Have your back foot
flat across the tail. As your nose approaches the wall,
push down on your tail slightly and slide your nose and
front wheels up onto the wall. As your front wheels slide

up the wall, push your back wheels up as well. As you come back down push down on your nose slightly so your back tail pops off the wall. Then you can ride back down without your tail jamming into the ground.

The secret is to keep your weight on your back leg as you slam into the wall and as you reach your maximum height, shift your weight to your front foot.

Wallie

This trick is best done on an angular parking block. Ride straight toward the block as if you were going to ollie it. Place your front foot right below the bottom bolts on your front truck. Put your back foot flat against the tail. When your nose nears the wall push down slight-

ly on your tail (without snapping) and slam your back
wheels up and into the curb. Most people lift up their
front wheels too high. Imagine riding up a steep bank.
Push your back wheels against and up the curb like you
are riding up a vert wall. When you reach the top, keep

45

The secret is to fight against your natural instinct of snapping the tail to clear the object.

sucking your back leg up and push down your front leg slightly so that you level off in the air. When you level out keep your knees bent for the landing.

Wallie Backside 180 Out

Ride straight up to the curb. Have your front foot over the top bolts of your front truck. Have your back foot flat across the tail. As your nose approaches the curb or barricade, push down on your tail and slide your nose and front wheels up the object. As your front wheels slide up,

push your back wheels up as well and level off in the air. As you level off, quickly turn your shoulders and head 180 and your lower body should follow.

The secret is to turn your shoulders quickly once you have leveled off in the air.

Wallie Frontside 180 Out

Ride straight up to the curb or block. Have your front foot over the top bolts of your front truck. Have your back foot flat across the tail. As your nose approaches the block, push down on your tail slightly and slide your nose and front wheels up the block. As your front wheels slide

up the curb or block, push your back wheels up as well and level off in the air. As you level off, turn your shoulders and head 180 and pull your front foot backwards so that you turn 180 and are riding fakie.

The secret is to turn your shoulders quickly once you have leveled off in the air.

Ollie Impossible

Place your front foot two inches below the bottom bolts on your front truck. The toes of your front foot should reach the middle of the board because you need to re-move your foot quickly to allow for the wraparound. Place your back foot flat across the tail of your board with the

ball of your foot placed right along the joint where the tail begins to bend. Hang your toes slightly off the edge of the tail to get a grip for the scoop. Scoop your back foot along the ground and straight forward, so the board pops up like a rocket. Push your foot forward and make a

The secret is to quickly scoop with your back foot.

small circle. The scoop and circular motion will cause the board to wrap around your back foot. When the board is completing the wraparound, bring your front foot back and place it on the front bolts of your truck.

Frontside Crailslide

Ride up with your front facing the ramp or bank. Approach the lip at a 30-degree angle. Pop an ollie when your front wheels are four inches from the lip. Ollie and turn your shoulders so that they make an intersecting T with the lip. Put pressure on your tail and press your back

61

wheels into the lip. When you slide, it will be your wheels and tail sliding together. As you are getting into tailslide, lean forward and grab the nose with your back hand and lean back slightly to push the slide. When you are nearing the end of your slide let go of your nose. Press down

The secret is to keep low on your board so that you can reach your nose as you get into tailslide.

and roll back into the bank.

Backside Crailslides

Ride with your back facing the ramp or bank. Approach the lip at a 30-degree angle. Ollie when your front wheels are four inches from the lip. Ollie and turn your shoulders to make an intersecting T with the lip. The natural tendency of backside tricks is to lean forward too much

and slip out. Press your tail down and push your back wheels into the lip. When you slide, it will be your wheels and tail sliding together. As you are getting into tailslide, lean forward and grab the nose with your back hand. Be prepared for the slide because backside tailslides tend to

The secret is to keep your upper body parallel with the coping so that it is easier to grab the nose, as well as keeping your balance when you slide.

slide a lot faster than frontside tailslides. When you are nearing the end of your slide, let go of your nose and press down with your front foot, rolling back into the transition or bank.

Pole Jam

Ride straight towards the pole, with the pole aimed between your two trucks. Place your front foot flat across
the board an inch below the bottom bolts on your front
truck. Put your back foot flat across the tail. When your
nose is about to hit the rail, lean back over the tail slight-

ly and push both feet into the pole. An extra hard push from your back foot will cause the momentum needed to grind up the pole. Bend your knees as you begin grinding up the pole and put very little weight on your front foot. Be sure that the rail stays in the middle of your trucks to

The secret is to pretend that you are riding up a steep bank ramp, so grind up with enough force.

maintain balance. Grind off the pole and keep sucking your back leg up, pushing down slightly on your front foot so that you level out in the air. Bend your legs as you descend for landing.

Ollie Late-Shuvit

Place your front foot flat across the board two inches below the bottom bolts on your front truck. Put your back
foot in the ollie position. Snap down on your tail and
slide your front foot up for an ollie, sucking both feet
up into your chest to get height. As the board reaches

the highest point, make sure the board is level. When it reaches the highest point, kick your back foot backward and your front foot forward causing the board to spin 180 (the board spinning 180 is what is called a shuvit.) As the board shuvits you will begin to descend. When the

The secret is kicking your feet once you have reached the highest point of your ollie.

board has finished spinning 180, put your feet back on the board and land.

Bigspin Flip

Place your back foot on the tail with your toes slightly hanging off the edge of your tail. Curl your toes to grip the board in order to scoop it properly. Place your front foot in a 40-degree angle with your heel hanging off slightly. Snap and scoop the tail with your back foot caus-

ing it to rotate 360 degrees. Use your front foot to flick the board as you begin the scoop. Once your front foot flicks the board, suck your legs up and turn a quick 180 while letting the board complete the 360 flip under your feet. As your body completes the 180, the board should

The secret is to think of it as a 360 flip. Once you have begun the 360 flip, quickly turn your body 180.

be done flipping. Place your feet back on the board keeping your knees bent.

Double Kickflip

Place your front foot at a 40-degree angle and your back foot in the ollie position with your heel raised and your weight on your toes and the ball of your foot. Snap your tail down and slide your front foot to the side. Give the board a good flick off the side and down. By flicking

and kicking downwards hard enough, the board will flip twice. As you flick and kick downwards, jump as high as you can. Once you descend, the board will have completed its double flip.

The secret is in timing your jump with the quickly rotating skateboard.

Frontside 180 No-Comply

Place your front foot over the bottom two bolts on your front truck. Place your back foot flat across the tail of your board. Begin the trick by turning your shoulders 90 degrees as if you were going to do a frontside 180. When your shoulders begin to turn, take your front foot off the

board and place it about 6 inches away from your board. Your foot will act like a pivot. As your front foot leaves the board, snap the tail with your back foot so the front wheels pop up and then swing your back foot around 180 guiding the board. As the board nears the completion of

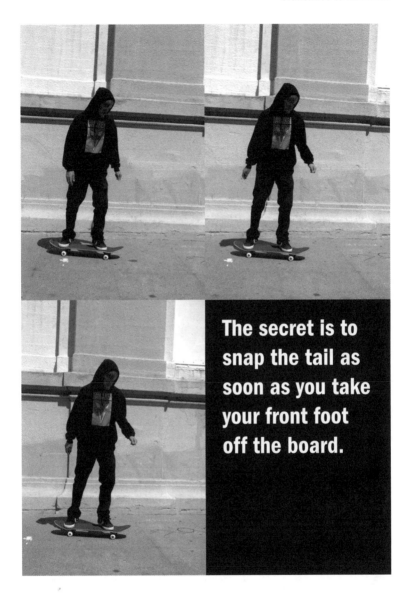

The secret is to snap the tail as soon as you take your front foot off the board.

the 180, put your front foot back on the board.

Varial Kickflip Body Varial

Place your front foot at a 40-degree angle and your back foot in the ollie position with your heel raised and your weight on your toes and the ball of your foot. Snap your tail down and scoop it backwards slightly so it spins 180. Slide your front foot up giving the board a good flick off

the side for the kickflip. As you scoop and flick the board it should begin spinning a varial kickflip. After the scoop and flick, turn your body 180 the opposite way. Keep your feet apart so you can land with both feet over the bolts.

The secret is to make sure you do a nice varial kickflip as you begin turning 180.

Switch Frontside Bigspin Heelflip

Place the ball of your back foot on the tail near the back corner where your heel normally goes when you do a switch ollie. Put your front foot in the middle of the board with your toes hanging off. Snap down on your back foot and scoop it away from your body so the board

begins to spin 360. When the board begins to turn, kick your front foot out and slightly forward. Kick the edge of the board with the ball of your front foot, causing it to flip. Rotate your shoulders once you snap down on the tail. As you turn 180 degrees, keep your knees sucked

The secret is to snap and scoop your back tail hard enough that it can complete the 360.

up into your chest. When your body completes the 180, your board should be completing its 360 flip. Place your feet back on the board and ride away.

Switch Backside Tailslide Bigspin Out

Place your back foot flat across the tail with your front foot covering the bottom bolts of your front truck. Come in at a 45-degree angle and snap your tail, sucking your feet up as you turn your shoulders backside. As you 180, land with your wheels pressed firmly into the curb and

your weight on the tail. You will begin to slide, be careful not to lean forward too much. As you begin to slow down on your slide or are nearing the end of the curb, kick your back foot slightly so that your board begins to spin. As the board spins, turn your body 90 degrees and

101

The secret is to perfect your switch backside 180's so you can get into solid switch backside tailslides.

wait for the board to fully rotate. Land on the board with your knees bent.

360 Double Flip

Place your back foot on the tail with your toes hanging slightly off the edge of your tail. Curl your toes to grip and scoop the board properly. Place your front foot in a 40-degree angle with your heel hanging off slightly. Snap and scoop the tail with your back foot, causing it to ro-

tate 360 degrees. Use your front foot to flick the board, but flick it extra hard so that the board flips twice.

The secret is to practice being able to balance the scooping of the tail with the flicking of your front foot.

Backside Bigspin

Place your front foot straight across the board two inches below the bottom bolts on your front truck. Place your back foot on the tail. Put your weight on the ball of your foot and toes and snap and scoop the tail so the board pops and spins a 360. As the board spins, you want to

catch it before you complete your 180. The longer the board is touching your feet the more you will know whether you will land it or not, and the more in control you will be.

The secret is to not lean forward too much as you land.

Frontside Bigspin

Place your front foot straight across the board two inches below the bottom bolts on your front truck. Have your toes hanging off the edge of the board. Place your back foot on the back corner of the tail so that you can snap and push with enough force to complete the 360. Put

113

your weight on the ball of your foot and toes. Snap and push the tail forward so the board pops and spins. As the board spins you want to catch it before you complete your 180. The longer the board is touching your feet the more you will know whether you will land it or not, and

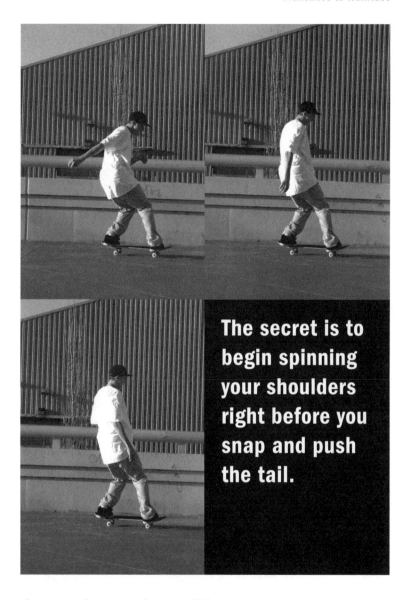

The secret is to begin spinning your shoulders right before you snap and push the tail.

the more in control you will be.

Bigspin Frontside Boardslide

Place your front foot straight across the board two inches below the bottom bolts on your front truck. Place the ball of your foot and toes in the center of the tail. Put your weight on the ball of your foot and toes. Snap the tail and scoop your tail backwards so the board pops and

spins 360. Turn your body so the rail is between your feet and catch the board before it lands on the rail. You will begin to slide. As you near the end, turn your shoulders so your board straightens out and ride away.

The secret is to look over your shoulder as you land on the rail so that you keep your balance as you slide.

Frontside Boardslide to Backside Nosegrind

Put your front foot under the bottom bolts on your front truck. Ollie onto the ledge, landing in a frontside boardslide. As you slide, lean forward on the nose raising your back trucks up. Push your front wheels and nose down and around on the curb, so that you are now in a back-

side nosegrind position. As you grind off the curb, shift your weight back towards your back leg so that you land balanced.

The secret is to quickly push down on your nose as you slide.

Frontside Boardslide Pop Over

Put your front foot under the bottom bolts on your front truck. Ollie onto the ledge, landing in frontside boardslide. As you slide, lean forward and push your nose down hard. As your nose goes down quickly, lift your back foot up and over the curb turning 90 degrees so

that you land riding away fakie.

The secret is the quick, jerky movement of pushing your nose down while quickly swinging your back leg up, over and around.

Kickflip Frontside Boardslide Pop Over

Place your front foot in the kickflip position. Snap your tail and flick your front foot off the edge and follow it around 90 degrees. Do it like a backside 180 kickflip. Catch the board above the rail or curb as it completes the flip and 90-degree turn and then land on the curb. Keep

your knees bent as you land on the curb. As you begin to slide, push your front foot down quickly and lift up your back truck so the board pops up and over. Turn 90 degrees in the process, riding away fakie.

The secret is to begin turning your shoulders right before you snap the tail.

Blunt Nosegrab

Ride up the bank with your front foot over the bolts of your front truck. Have your back foot flat across the tail. As your front wheels near the top (also called the lip), lean back slightly and push your board up until you feel your back wheels and tail lock into the blunt posi-

135

tion. As you lock into blunt, snap the tail once you grab the nose of your board with your front arm. Pull the board up and back, jumping up and back together with the board. As you come back into the bank your back wheels will hit first and then your front wheels. Keep

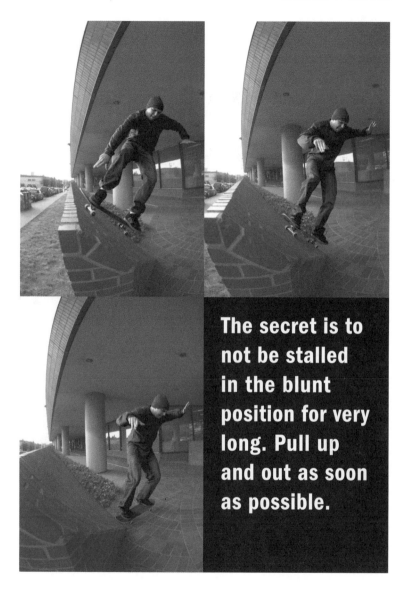

The secret is to not be stalled in the blunt position for very long. Pull up and out as soon as possible.

your body low and your legs bent for better balance.

Kickflip Feeble

Place your front foot at a 40-degree angle and your back foot in the ollie position with your heel raised and weight on the ball of your foot and toes. Snap your tail down as you approach the rail. As you snap, slide your front foot up and sideways, giving the board a flick. As you flick

your board, it should spin a level kickflip. Once the board reaches your feet the back truck should be aimed to hit the rail. As you land on the rail, keep all your weight over your back leg so the back truck grinds.

The secret is being able to do nice kickflips and being able to keep your weight on your back truck as you land.

Nollie Bigspin Boardslide

Put your weight on the ball and toes of your front foot. Place your back foot an inch below the bottom bolts of your back truck. Snap your nose hard and scoop your front foot back slightly so the board spins. As you jump up and the board is rotating, turn your shoulders 90

degrees and catch the board with your feet before it lands on the rail. Land with the rail in the middle of the board and slide to the end of the rail.

The secret is to learn how to do nice nollie bigspins so that you maintain your balance when you get on a rail or curb.

Frontside Boardslide 270 Out

Ride up to the curb keeping a distance of 10 inches. Put your front foot an inch below the bottom bolts on your front truck. Place your back foot in the ollie position. Ollie and turn your body and board 90-degrees with your front wheels landing on the curb. As your slide nears the

end, push down on your front leg and begin to turn your shoulders quickly. At the same time pull your back foot around as you spin. How hard you turn will determine the amount you spin. Spin hard enough so that you complete the 270 out.

The secret is to approach the curb with speed and be sure to push down on your nose and front leg before beginning to rotate.

Nosebonk

Approach the object as if to ollie over it. Have your front foot covering the front bolts on your front truck. Ollie, and as you rise, instead of leveling out the board, push your nose down so that your back wheels are elevated higher than your front wheels. Land with your front

wheels on the object as if it were a nose manual. As the wheels touch down, push your board forward so that you clear the object without your back wheels touching.

The secret is to push the board forward quickly as soon as your front wheels touch down.

Nosebonk 180

Approach the object as if to ollie over it. Have your front foot covering the front bolts on your front truck. Ollie, and as you rise, instead of leveling out the board, push your nose down so that your back wheels are elevated higher than your front wheels. Land with your

155

front wheels on the object as if it were a nose manual. As the wheels touch down, push your board forward and turn your shoulders 180. Pivot off the object and complete a 180.

The secret is to use your front wheels as a pivot once they touch down on the object.

About the author

Evan Goodfellow has been skateboarding since 1988. His sponsors have included Vans Shoes, Ambiguous Clothing, 88 Shoes, Zion Skateboards, and Ninetimes Boardshop. Evan has written four other instructional skateboarding books. His most recent books include an instructional skateboarding book called *Skateboarding: Rails, Rails, Rails* and a fictional skateboard book entitled *Skateboard Daze at Hollywood High*.

About the photographer

Tadashi Yamaoda loves to skate and loves shooting skateboard action. For more info and a look at some of his other work, please visit www.tadashiphoto.com

Magazines

The Skateboard Mag

142 N. Cedros Ste. B,
Solana Beach, CA 92075

www.theskateboardmag.com

This magazine was started by former staff members from *Transworld Skateboarding* magazine in an attempt to purify skateboarding from the over-commercialization they felt was taking place at *Transworld Skateboarding*. The quality of the magazine and both the writing and photos make it a top choice among skateboard magazines.

Transworld Skateboarding Magazine

TransWorld Media
353 Airport Rd
Oceanside, CA 92054

www.skateboarding.com

Transworld Skateboarding has been around for a very long time and has always produced good interviews and good photos. The quality of the magazine over the years has helped make it my second choice.

Thrasher Skateboard Magazine

High Speed Productions Inc.
1303 Underwood Ave
San Francisco, CA 94124

www.thrashermagazine.com

Thrasher magazine is based out of San Francisco and often features spots and skateboarders that aren't featured in *Transworld* which brings an added flavor to the skateboard world. This magazine also features cool, up and coming bands, or long established hard core bands.

Color Magazine
Four Corner Publishing Inc.
321 Railway Street
Studio 105
Vancouver, BC
Canada
V6A 1A4

www.colormagazine.ca

This magazine is a new artsy skateboard magazine coming from Canada. It's high quality paper and pictures make it an enjoyable read. The Canadian flavor brings an extra unique taste showing spots and riders that often do not appear in American skateboard magazines.

Skateboard Websites

The Berrics
This website is run by Steve Berra and Eric Koston. It is constantly updated and is the best skateboard website out there.

www.theberrics.com

Evan's Top 5 Sites

Board Sites

Girl Skateboards
www.girlskateboards.com

Zero Skateboards
www.zeroskateboards.com

Real Skateboards
www.realskateboards.com

Plan B Skateboards
www.planbskateboarding.com

Cliché Skateboards
www.clicheskate.com

Truck Sites

Royal Trucks
www.royalskateboardtruck.com

Independent Trucks
www.independenttrucks.com

Venture Trucks
www.venturetrucks.net

Thunder Trucks
www.thundertrucks.com

Destructo Trucks
www.destructotrucks.com

Shoe Sites

Circa Shoes
www.circafootwear.com

Fallen Shoes
www.fallenfootwear.com

DC Shoes
www.dcshoecousa.com

IPATH Shoes
www.ipath.com

More Skateboard Books from Veva Skateboarding Books

**Skateboard Daze
at Hollywood High**

**Skateboarding:
Rails, Rails, Rails**